Welcomed *by* Name

Our Child's Baptism

Peg Bowman

LOYOLAPRESS.

LOYOLAPRESS.

3441 N. Ashland Avenue
Chicago, Illinois 60657
(800) 621-1008
LoyolaEducationGroup.org

NIHIL OBSTAT
Reverend Charles R. Meyer, S.T.D.
Censor Deputatus
February 18, 2003

IMPRIMATUR
Most Reverend Raymond E. Goedert, M.A., S.T.L., J.C.L.
Vicar General
Archdiocese of Chicago
February 19, 2003

The *Nihil Obstat* and *Imprimatur* are official declarations that a book is free of doctrinal and moral error. No implication is contained therein that those who have granted the *Nihil Obstat* and *Imprimatur* agree with the content, opinions, or statements expressed. Nor do they assume any legal responsibility associated with publication.

Acknowledgments for quoted material and photographs appear on page 30, which is to be considered a continuation of the copyright page.

Cover and Interior Design: Judine O'Shea

ISBN: 0-8294-1798-2

Contents

Bathed in Grace

It is wonderful that you have chosen to have your baby baptized.

Karl Rahner, a Jesuit priest, once said, "The world is bathed in grace." Think about what that means. God is with us in every time and every place, giving us gifts, showering us with grace. God bathes us and our world in grace.

In the saving waters of Baptism, your baby will be bathed in grace and become a child of God. What a joy it is to welcome a new baby by birth or by adoption! What an added joy to welcome a new child of God through Baptism! Your family's blessing becomes a blessing for the Church and for the world.

This book has ideas and images to help you prepare for this important step in your family's life. Use it both for writing your thoughts and prayers while you await your child's birth and for recording memories of the Baptism itself. Try out its suggestions for ways to help your child and your family grow in God's grace.

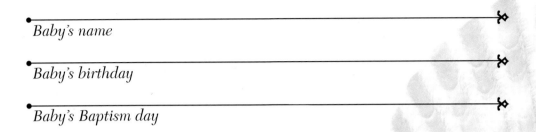

Baby's name

Baby's birthday

Baby's Baptism day

Place your own photos in
this space.

Place your own photos in
this space.

Us During Pregnancy

Our Baby at Birth

What Does the Church Ask of You?

At the beginning of the Rite of Baptism the celebrant, usually a priest or a deacon, will ask "What do you ask of God's Church for this child?"

You may answer, "Baptism." You may also use other words, such as "faith" or "the grace of Christ" or "entrance into the Church" or "eternal life." You may even use your own words in keeping with these responses. Use the opposite page for writing ideas about how you might respond to this question.

Now, however, turn the question around: "What does God's Church ask of you?"

The answer given in the Baptism liturgy is that you are to train your child in the practice of the faith, to bring your child up to keep God's commandments by loving God and neighbor, and to see that the divine life in your child is kept safe.

Just as your baby looks to you for food, shelter, and love in order to grow strong and healthy, this little one also needs you for spiritual growth—to nourish faith, to offer guidance, and to provide moral training. Through your human love your child will experience God's love. What an honor!

The Church asks you to be the best teacher and Christian role model you can be. Would you want it any other way?

We want our baby baptized because:

My Family—A Church

"This cluttered, noisy, confused place—a church?" you ask.

Yes indeed. The Second Vatican Council called the family a domestic church and parents the "first preachers of the faith" (*Dogmatic Constitution on the Church*, 11).

Amid the clutter and confusion and personalities and gifts that make up your home, your child will receive the first taste of love and the first experience of God.

So where do you begin? With prayer. Pray for and with your family. You do not need many words. Two of the best prayer words are *please* and *thanks*. A third word is *love*. You will find natural prayer moments for the family each day—waiting times, mealtimes, travel times, bedtimes—and there will be others if you watch for them. Use your own words to give thanks and praise to God. If parents use and enjoy prayer times, children will too.

Begin now—with this baby. Even during pregnancy, offer prayers of petition and thanks and love. After your baby's birth, softly say or sing prayers as you feed, diaper, comfort, or play with this new family member. Your baby will not understand your words at first but will certainly feel your love.

Write a prayer for your baby.

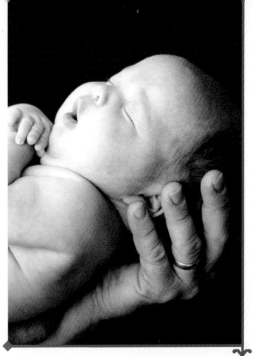

See what love the Father has bestowed on us that we may be called the children of God. Yet so we are.

1 John 3:1

7

Belonging to the Church

Belonging to the whole Church extends beyond the domestic church of your family. In the Church we are all connected; we are all members of the one Body of Christ. This belonging to Christ and to the Church comes with important rights and responsibilities. As you bring your child for Baptism, you are saying that you want these rights and responsibilities for this child. Baptism is much more than a one-time ritual. You are setting your child on a lifelong path.

Belonging to the Church gives us these rights:

❖ to gather with the assembly of believers for worship and prayer

❖ to hear the Word of God proclaimed

❖ to participate in the sacraments

We also have responsibilities as Church members. We must consciously live as Christians:

- ✧ seeking God in prayer both public and private

- ✧ working to build up the Church

- ✧ living the message of the gospel in our daily lives

- ✧ doing what we can to bring all things and all people to Christ

What do you hope Church membership will mean for you and your child?

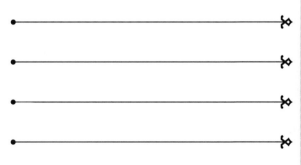

Why Baptism?

It all starts with being made new. Just as physical birth marks the beginning of a child's physical life, the new birth in Baptism marks the beginning of a child's Christian life. Both take place in this world that God has created. Without Baptism there can be no sharing in other sacraments. Baptism is called "the gateway to life in the Spirit" (*Catechism of the Catholic Church,* 1213).

Baptism will not change your baby's appearance, but it will change what really matters most. No longer an "outsider," this child will be an "insider," a member of Christ's Body. Your baby's whole being will be permanently marked as a baptized Christian. This one-time sacrament can never be repeated or taken away.

Your child will enter into a life of grace: God the Father, the Son, and the Holy Spirit will live in your little one in a new way.

Grace and Sin

During the Baptism liturgy, the celebrant will say to your child: "[Name], the Christian community welcomes you with great joy. In its name I claim you for Christ our Savior by the sign of his cross."

Being claimed for Christ is being claimed by God. God's grace is first. From all eternity God desires to share divine life. The Son of God became a human being to share God's life and God's grace with us in a very real way.

Christ's Baptism,
John Nava, 2002,
tapestry at the Cathedral of
Our Lady of the Angels

12

Like every human being born since our first parents (with the exception of Christ himself and Mary, the Mother of God), your baby is born into the human condition. Sadly for everyone, sin is part of that condition.

Original sin is part of human life. No one can avoid it. But Jesus Christ has overcome sin and evil. No one need be trapped forever in sin. Jesus lived, died, rose from the dead, and ascended to the Father to free us from death and sin. In Baptism we receive that salvation in Christ.

Your baby will be claimed for Christ and washed clean of original sin in Baptism.

Sacraments
Signs That Are Real

How can we know anything about God or the life of a person? Probably the best way to know things is to experience them—seeing, touching,  hearing, tasting. Experiencing things through the senses is part of being human. God communicates to us in these very human ways. Through the Church we have tangible, physical signs that not only tell us about God but also manifest God's presence to us. We call these very special signs *sacraments*. They are God's mighty works.

Any sign points to something real, but sacraments do more than merely point. Sacraments *cause* what they signify. The Church's seven sacraments give us seven ways to experience God, to receive God's life, to meet God.

The Church itself is lovingly described as the sacrament of communion that brings us to Christ (*Catechism of the Catholic Church*, 1108).

Because the Son of God became a human being, all of human life can point to God. We can find something sacramental about many things in our everyday lives. Being a parent can be sacramental.

How has becoming a parent helped you encounter God, experience God, meet God?

Passing on a Heritage

It should not surprise you that the Church takes seriously the choice of your child's name. Your child will carry this name through life into eternity.

Have you named this baby for a relative or another special person? Did you choose the name for its sound or its meaning? This name used in Baptism may be a traditional Christian one. It may also be a name of regional usage as long as it is not incompatible with Christian faith. At Baptism, the Church adds some Christian interpretation to this given name.

Why did you choose your child's name? What role model or virtue is connected to this name?

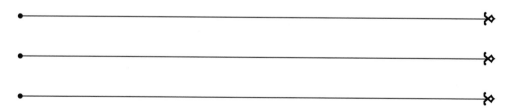

Each godparent you choose provides another Christian role model. It is an honor and a responsibility to be a godparent. You may choose a godmother, or a godfather, or both, who will have a special and lasting bond with your child.Godparents have a public role during the liturgy of Baptism and thereafter are to stand ready to help with your child's spiritual and social formation in the years to come.

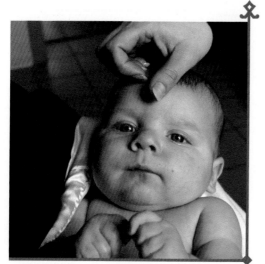

Whom have you chosen as godparent(s) for this child? Why did you select each one for this honor and duty?

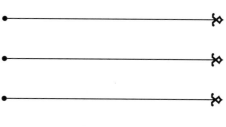

Signs of Baptism
Welcoming and Anointing

There will be much to notice at your baby's Baptism. Each sign and symbol and each ritual action is important and has a special meaning.

- **The gathered community** signifies the whole Church, standing to welcome this new member and assenting to the profession of our faith.

- **Signing with the cross** is one of the first ritual actions. You will be invited to join the celebrant in tracing the Sign of the Cross on your baby's forehead to claim this new member for Christ. Godparents, family members, and parishioners may be invited to do the same.

- **Anointing** occurs twice in the Baptism of small children. Before the immersion or pouring of water, the baby will be anointed on the breast with the *oil of catechumens*. This first anointing calls on Christ to strengthen the one who will be baptized.

Later the baby will be anointed on the head with *chrism*. This second anointing—with sweet-smelling chrism, which takes its name from Christ—joins the newly baptized to Christ who is Priest, Prophet, and King. Because of Christ, the newly baptized will be strengthened to live a life that is priestly, prophetic, and royal.

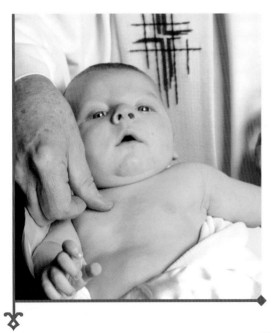
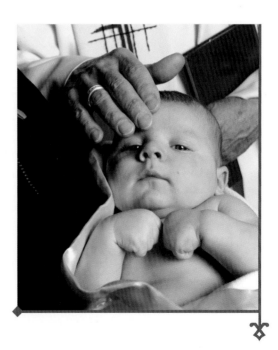

Signs of Baptism
New Life in Christ

Other signs of Baptism may be more familiar to you:

+ **Water** is the central symbol of this sacrament. The Church wants a generous use of water, whether the sacrament is by immersion, which is preferred, or by pouring. In this bath your child will be washed free from sin. In this bath your child will be buried with Christ but then raised up to new life in him. Even the prayer of blessing over the water will remind us of its power. Water can give life, save life, and take away life. In the waters of Baptism, sin is destroyed; new life emerges; all is clean, refreshed, and new.

+ **The baptismal garment** is provided by the family. It may be something new or something that has been used by the family for generations. It is usually white in color. This baptismal garment is an outward sign of your child's new life in Christ.

The lighted candle signifies the light of Christ to be kept burning bright all through life. The Easter candle burns throughout the Baptism liturgy. Your baby's own candle will be lit from this Easter candle. Keep and use this candle for special occasions to show how future celebrations are connected to this Baptism day.

The Rite of Baptism
Before You Approach the Font

Whether your child is baptized during Sunday Mass or at another time on Sunday, the liturgy will follow the same basic outline.

✢   The celebrant meets you at the entrance to the church or baptistry and asks, "What name do you give your child?" and "What do you ask of God's Church for your child?" Your answer is "Baptism" or "faith" or "the grace of Christ" or something similar. Look back at what you wrote on page 5. More questions will make sure that you and the godparents understand your responsibilities.

❖ The celebrant claims your child for Christ by tracing the Sign of the Cross on the baby's forehead and inviting you and others to do the same.

❖ The Liturgy of the Word is next. Scripture readings and the homily lead all those assembled to a deeper understanding of the mystery of Baptism. Intercessions with a short litany of the saints, which may include your child's patron saint, follow.

❖ The celebrant anoints the baby's breast with the oil of catechumens for protection from evil and for strengthening in Christ.

❖ All process to the font.

The Rite of Baptism
At the Font and After

✥ At the font the celebrant blesses the water. In this blessing we recall God's mighty deeds, God's grace, and the power of Baptism in the life of the Church.

✥ The parents and godparents renounce sin and profess faith on behalf of the child. The assembly gives its assent to this profession in spoken word or song.

- In the saving waters of the font, your child is baptized "in the name of the Father, and of the Son, and of the Holy Spirit." Your child is immersed three times or has water poured upon him or her three times.

- The celebrant anoints the crown of your child's head with chrism.

- You or the godparents dress this child in the baptismal garment, which is an outward sign of Christian dignity.

- A godparent lights the child's candle from the Easter candle after the celebrant says, "Receive the light of Christ."

- A prayer for the opening of the ears and mouth to hear Christ's word and proclaim his faith may be prayed, at the discretion of the minister.

- Mass now continues in the usual way. If Baptism is celebrated outside Mass, everyone processes to the altar and prays the Lord's Prayer, and the liturgy concludes with a special blessing and dismissal.

What if a newborn is in danger of death? In an emergency, anyone may baptize, using ordinary water and saying the words "I baptize you in the name of the Father, and of the Son, and of the Holy Spirit." If the baby lives, the Church does not "rebaptize." Instead, the child is brought to the church, and the rest of the rite is carried out there.

First Teachers of This Child

You promised to bring up this child in the Catholic faith. How do you plan to do this? Plan? Yes. Now is a good time to plan. In fact, now is the best time to begin.

Pray together as a family. Use traditional prayers, prayers from books, and prayers in your own words. Select some religious music tapes or CDs. Play and sing along with them at home and in the car.

Get a children's Bible and begin to read stories from it now, even before your child can understand them. You and other family members will enjoy their simple messages. Use this or a big family Bible for recording the names and special dates of each family member.

Celebrate religious anniversaries, especially Baptism days. Bake a cake; light the child's baptismal candle; pray and sing in thanksgiving.

Invite godparents to these and other special events. Encourage them to spend time with your child. They can be supportive, interested adults, especially as a child grows older.

How will you share your faith with your child?

$\star$—Models of Christianity—$\star$

Your child will notice everything you do. You are a role model whether you feel up to the task or not! The formation of a good Christian conscience is important in bringing up a child in the faith. Teaching the difference between right and wrong cannot wait until grade school; it begins as soon as your child understands the words *yes* and *no*.

How will you teach your child about the consequences of actions? How will you demonstrate forgiveness, and how will you ask for forgiveness yourself?

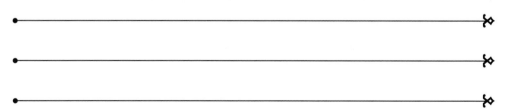

What do you want this child to learn from you about our faith? What do you need to do to help that happen?

Begin early to take your child to Mass. It is most important that your child see you practicing your faith—participating in Mass and the other sacraments, praying at home, taking part in the life of the community, giving aid to those in need, and making good moral decisions.

You have been chosen to be this child's first and best teacher. God bless you in this important role.

Acknowledgments (continued from page ii)

Text

Scripture excerpts are taken from the *New American Bible with Revised New Testament and Psalms* copyright © 1991, 1986, 1970 Confraternity of Christian Doctrine, Inc., Washington D.C. Used with permission. All rights reserved. No part of the *New American Bible* may be reproduced by any means without permission in writing from the copyright owner.

English translation of the *Catechism of the Catholic Church* for the United States of America copyright © 1994, United States Catholic Conference, Inc.—Libreria Editrice Vaticana. English translation of the *Catechism of the Catholic Church: Modifications from the Editio Typica* copyright © 1997, United States Catholic Conference, Inc.—Libreria Editrice Vaticana. Used with permission.

Photographs

Photo page positions: top (t), middle (m), bottom (b), right (r), left (l)
Cover: Phil Martin Photography
Phil Martin Photography **ii, iii, 5, 11, 13, 17(b), 19, 21, 23.** Getty images: Charles Gupton **6**, Andre Gallant **7**, Luc Beziat **14**, Barbara Peacock **15**, Justin Pumfrey **17(t),** China Tourism Press **26**, Bruce Ayres **27**, David Young-Wolff **29(t),** Fischer-Thatcher **29(br),** Barros & Barros **29(bm),** Andy Sacks **29(bl).** Steve J. P. Liang/News-Leader **8.** © Lawrence Migdale **9.** Property of John Nava and the Archdiocese of Los Angeles. Used by permission. All rights reserved **12.** Chapel of St. Ignatius, Seattle University/Anil Kapahi **18, 22.** The Crosiers/Gene Plaisted OSC **20.** Diane Eichhold **24.** All other photograhs from Loyola Press.